New & Selected Poems

CLIFF YATES was born in Birmingham and grew up in Birmingham and Kidderminster. He left school at 16 for the printing factory and did various jobs before returning to full time education. He taught English at Maharishi School, where his students were renowned for winning poetry competitions. Awards for his poetry include the Fenton Aldeburgh First Collection Prize, the Poetry Business Book & Pamphlet Competition, and an Arts Council England Writers Award. He wrote *Jumpstart Poetry in the Secondary School* during his time as Poetry Society poet-in-residence. A hugely experienced writing tutor, he is a former Royal Literary Fund Fellow at Aston University.

New & Selected Poems
Cliff Yates

smith|doorstop

the poetry business

Published 2023
by The Poetry Business
Campo House,
54 Campo Lane,
Sheffield S1 2EG
www.poetrybusiness.co.uk

Copyright © Cliff Yates 2023
The moral rights of the author have been asserted.
ISBN 978-1-914914-59-1

All rights reserved.
Without limiting the rights under copyright reserved above, no part of this publication may be reproduced, storied in or introduced into a retrieval system, or transmitted, in any form or by any means (electronic, mechanical, photocopying, recording or otherwise), without the prior written permission of both the copyright owner and the above publisher of this book.

Designed & typeset by Utter.
Printed by Imprint Digital

British Library Cataloguing-in-Publication Data.
A catalogue record for this book is available from the British Library.

Smith|Doorstop is a member of Inpress
www.inpressbooks.co.uk.

Distributed by BookSource, 50 Cambuslang Road,
Cambuslang Investment Park, Glasgow G32 8NB.

The Poetry Business gratefully acknowledges the support
of Arts Council England.

Contents

from *Henry's Clock* (1999)

- 11 Tonight in Kidderminster
- 13 Waiting for Caroline
- 14 Ferret
- 15 Apples
- 16 Hank
- 17 Leswell Street
- 18 Poem on the Decline of the Carpet Industry
- 19 Henry's Clock
- 20 Oakworth
- 21 On the Difficulty of Learning Chinese
- 22 Clara
- 23 Playing for Time
- 24 Bricks in the Snow
- 25 Borth
- 26 Telescope
- 27 The Day the Lawnmower Caught Fire
- 28 *from* The Pond Poems
- 30 Get Me Flowers
- 31 Meeting the Family
- 32 Naked, the Philosopher
- 33 *from* 14 Ways of Listening to the Archers

from *Frank Freeman's Dancing School* (2009)

- 35 Lighthouse
- 36 Locked In
- 37 Thank You for the Postcard I Read it
- 38 Emergency Rations are Tasting Better and Better

40	Fishing
41	Leaves Are Just Thin Wood
42	Daglingworth Blues
43	On the Third Day
44	Day Breaks as a Petrol Station
45	L'Hermitage and a Bird
46	Hôtel de l'Angleterre
47	Shoes
48	Would you listen to the safety instructions please
49	At the Smell of the Old Dog
50	Apple Trees in a Gale
51	Baldwin Road
52	New White Bike
53	Yes
54	Kidderminster-on-Sea
55	Vienna
56	The Poem
57	Boggle Hole
58	The Science of Predictive Astrology
59	Snow

from *Jam* (2016)

60	Chez Marianne
61	Life Studies
62	Alt St Johann
63	Easter
64	The Chinese Girls Played Cards
65	Bike, Rain
66	Spade Bucket Apple
67	February, Colden Valley
68	I Met my Friend

69	Bike Ride
70	Just Before You Taste It
71	Shakespeare and Company
72	Bar Billiards
73	Fifteen
74	Apprentice
75	The Bowling Green
76	Chapter Twenty, Leonard Cohen
77	Born in Handsworth
78	There's a Full-Size Snooker Table in the YMCA Furniture Shop
79	Pilates
80	*from* Riversound
82	The Lesson
83	Blue Sofa
84	How do you fly in your dreams?
85	Gate
86	The End of the World Again
87	Rain on the Conservatory Roof
88	Lighthouse III
90	Travis Perkins

from *Birmingham Canal Navigation* (2020)

91	Birmingham Canal
92	Lifting
93	Collapse: Barry Flanagan at the Ikon Gallery
94	Bank Holiday
95	Spitfires were built in Castle Bromwich
97	Red Sky Lift
98	I've Just Invented the Tai Chi Sprout Stalk Form
100	5:15 p.m. February 9th 2017
101	A Thing to Do

102	Swimming Pool
103	Black Sabbath Bridge
104	Sky Blues Bus
106	Dog

from *Another Last Word* (2021)

107	*from* Another Last Word
110	Taxman

New Poems

111	Tonight We're Showing a Film
112	Fish Street
113	Eagle Special Investigator
114	Phil and the Tension Wire
115	Meeting the Train
116	Bastille Day
117	Nightingale
118	October
119	Acknowledgements

For Gillian

Tonight in Kidderminster

begins under streetlights and their word is speed.
Two of them, chewing gum with their mouths open,
thumbs in their pockets and feet tapping.

The tall one sees me first, sees the hat. This hat
goes with the hair, the desert boots and jeans,
the shabby raincoat and ripped gold lining,

it goes with the sky before rain and just after,
and with one unforgettable night on Kinver Edge,
eight of us in the back of a Mini Van.

This hat is my dad's and I wouldn't sell it for fifty pounds.

✷

They chased me for the hat and lost, turned left
into another story. Fiction.
It begins up an entry, trembling hands

full of someone's prescription.
Eyes that are needles
sewing the hem on tomorrow's shroud.

✷

Or gramophone needles. The first record
is Stravinsky's *Soldier's Tale.*
The devil's guest Private Faust
has forgotten the silent princess.

He hums along to the drum solo
and dreams only of the fiddle
he traded for a book, words
he could not read, words he can't remember.

*

Next it's *4' 33'*,
a bootleg of David Tudor
live in Woodstock, New York 1952.

The duff tape missed the rain
on the roof, traffic in the distance,
the people angrily rising and leaving

but detected the silence, four years
in the making. Listen. No
sound but the lid of the piano.

Tonight in Kidderminster our audience
is the night. The agitated stars cough less
and less discreetly, by the third movement

programmes flutter like moths. Barely visible
to the naked eye, the devil jigs
to the soldier's fiddle while the silent princess

wheels the plough across the night sky
and the pole star stays where it is.

Waiting for Caroline

Outside Readings on Blackwell Street,
bikes in one window, jokes in this one:
nail through your finger, Frankenstein,
invisible ink. She looked great
behind the gym at dinner time.
Her friends were in the long jump pit
out of sight of the dinner ladies,
holding down Andy and giving him love
bites. Outside Fletcher's, Mr Fletcher
humps potatoes, sings in Italian. She's late.

I've been set up, like Cary Grant
in *North by North West*
                          I'll hear it
before I see it, the crop duster
out of the sun above the multi-storey
dipping dangerously over the Seven Stars.
I'll make it to the Red Cross on Silver Street,
under the ambulance, hands over my ears ...
On the way home, the fat man in the black suit
will climb on the Stourport bus with his cello.

I imagine her coming round the corner
by the Riverboat, she's run from the bus stop
but she's not sweating, she's smiling
like the girl in the Flake advert.

I'll tell John I didn't turn up
and if Frog says anything I'll hit him.

Ferret

My ferret is a very British ferret,
shy and retiring unless provoked.
I keep him in a special case,
strapped to the petrol tank
of my BSA 500. This gives me
a special feeling, like wellingtons
with a dinner jacket, or pumps.

I tried to feed him sardines but he wouldn't.
I think he's got a hormone imbalance.
He chewed through the lawnmower
cable once. If it had been switched on
it would have served him right.
Then he found the bonemeal in the shed.
I heard him cough from the greenhouse and my wife
nearly fell off the ladder. The river's flooded.
It hasn't stopped raining since Christmas.

Apples

The children won't sleep, we give them apples.
There is hardly enough light for these strange signs,
unfamiliar road markings, the distinction between
mile and kilometre. Our headlights find a farmhouse ...

Men and women in the loft, hide inside barrels
with last year's apples, praying the rats keep still.
The young officer in the room below
slowly raises a Luger to the ceiling
and fires at random, here and here. Blood
drips on his outstretched finger.
His men's boots clatter on wooden steps.

From barrels, hands push through to light,
apples bounce and roll across the floor,
machine guns rattle and grow hot.
Some stay crouched among the harvest,
breathing the sweet smell of bruised fruit.

Our youngest is so tired she can hardly
keep awake, let alone eat. She chews slowly
as if she is not used to eating,
hasn't eaten for a long time, has forgotten.

Hank
(for Brendan Cleary)

Woke up this morning in Arizona,
a filling station on the highway,
under someone's pick-up, dismantling the gear-box
which is a joke
because I'm the kind of bloke
who starts looking
for the left-handed hammer.

My name is Hank, I smoke roll-ups,
call you Bud and have a wife called Gloria
who hangs endless items of clothing
on the washing line out front
when she's not in the house
singing along to Country and Western
on the radio.

Men just turn up and say, 'How's it going Hank?'
I hammer repeatedly on the silencer
pretending I can't hear,
hoping they will go away
and thinking, 'Who the hell is this?
What does he know
about me that I don't know?'

I inspected the washing, worked out
that we have eight children
between two and sixteen. Also,
judging from the patches
on the jeans and shirts
and the state of repair of the house,
we're not rich. And judging from the way
I'm going at this gear box with a monkey wrench,
not likely to be.

Leswell Street

The end of a long night out, roe and chips
and batter bits settling well on a couple of pints
before the long walk home up Birmingham Road.
The house asleep, all the noise inside my head,
voices, pictures ...
                    Voices, pictures, the brow
of the hill in the rear-view mirror, foot off
the accelerator, cruising downhill in neutral
missing the signposts. At least the tyres
are new, to me anyway, part-worn
from Germany. Off a wreck, probably

like the one by the roundabout,
flames and black smoke pouring out
of the driver's seat, the man in the suit
carrying a briefcase, signalling the traffic
to take a different route because
at any moment the petrol tank

Poem on the Decline of the Carpet Industry

You have given up smoking
and wander about the house in your vest.
You're working on a novel called *Breakfast*.
You get up early like Ernest Hemmingway
and try to write a thousand words a day
on the typewriter but don't take time off
to fish in the Gulf Stream.
The most athletic thing you do is shave
though some nights you go for a long walk with a pram
that you fill with firewood from the building site.
The free newspaper comes in useful for lighting the fire.

Your parties are legendary:
videos of *Dixon of Dock Green*
on a huge black and white television
to the sound of Captain Beefheart, Chicken Shack
and Duster Bennett live at Frank Freeman's.
Let's applaud the perfect moment,
George himself saluting the camera
under the famous black and white blue lamp
to the opening bars of 'Autumn's Child.'

Henry's Clock

Henry's alarm clock stops ringing when you shout.
He likes to set it for one minute
and shout 'STOP!' It is satisfying

but not intelligent. If you shout
'CARRY ON!' it stops. It does not discriminate
between happiness, anger and despair.

If you like, you can shout
'THE RIDERS ARE TRAMPLING THE NIGHT
ON THEIR TERRIBLE SHINING HORSES!'

Oakworth

December. It's been dark all afternoon.
Telescope over his shoulder, my brother
climbs gingerly the steps of his new garden.
We wait in the light from the kitchen,
watching the beam of his pencil torch.
The kids are so patient. It's unbelievably cold.
'Turn off your torch, stand here, that's right
not too close. You don't need your glasses.'

He shows us Jupiter with its bands of clouds
and Saturn with its rings and moons.
Jewels. They're so small and intense
I could watch them forever.
The motor hums as the Earth turns.

Mum climbs the treacherous steps
to see for herself, holding onto my arm.
'However does he manage?' she says.
She's staying for Christmas. I leave her on the sofa
watching television in front of the gas fire.
Driving back over the Pennines it starts to snow.

On the Difficulty of Learning Chinese

My father met my horse when he was 19.
She was 12 but you only had to see them together.
He was handsome and she was incomparably beautiful.

She also had the most wonderful singing voice.
Father said she could sing the stars out of the sky.
My friends would come round just to be with her.

She was like a second horse to them.
When I was 11 she gave me my horse scarf.
Such a wonderful texture: cool in summer, warm in winter.

She made it from an old shirt belonging to my father.
He would never throw anything away.
But he was so angry. It was the first and last time

that I ever heard him use the word linen.

Clara

'Sweet Sir?' 'No thank you, I've just eaten
a little boy.' He stands at the classroom door,

rubbing together big hands. 'Poetry tomorrow
Clara, poetry!' Clara has other plans.

She's seeing Andy who's doing Sociology
and English at the college. Saturday

he took her on the terraces, Villa Park.
She stood behind him, warming her hands

in the back pockets of his Wranglers.
Later they shared a hot dog at the fair,

started at either end, met in the middle.
On the bus home they sat upstairs at the back

smoking French cigarettes. He cupped both hands
around her goldfish in its plastic bag,

she peeped through the cracks, wanting it to sleep
in the pink dark. Tomorrow it's his place,

his mum's out for the day. He'll read her
his essay on 'The Crisis of Identity of the Post

Industrial British Working Class.' They'll lie
in front of the electric fire

listening to Van Morrison. Later, upstairs
they'll run a warm bath, set the goldfish free.

Playing for Time

Blindfolded, arms out like sleepwalkers,
we stumble down the corridor, pretending
to be blind for English. In the toilets we skid
on wet tiles, make ghost noises, pretend to be drunk.

Next door it's trigonometry.
Mr Russell draws a ladder on the board,
talks about window cleaners, tangents,
flexes his cane and calls it George.

Here in RE the school chaplain
has just smacked the wrong boy on the head
for making a high-pitched whining noise
while he was dictating notes on Jeremiah.

He's not having a good day.
We have hidden his cane
behind the wall map of Jerusalem.
Earlier, a grain of rice from my biro, aimed

at the four-inch wooden cross balanced
on the bookcase, landed on his mark book
in a pool of spit. He made me empty my pockets.
I had enough rice to make a pudding.

Over the bike sheds the sun
shines through the fog like a Trebor mint.

Bricks in the Snow

After the printing factory, A-levels
at college. For six weeks
I didn't know where I was.
The sociology lecturer told us
to call him Rob.

'That's why you're here,'
he says, grinning,
'so you won't have to do that.'
Outside, builders
are humping bricks in the snow.

A lad throws bricks to his mate
up on the scaffolding.
They fly red
through falling snow
every one caught clean.

When I go back, Rob is fatter
than I remember. Beer.

Borth

We're woken up by tearing grass, cow breath
and the sun, orange through the walls of the tent.
We swim in summer rain, the sea warm
as bath water. The farmer drives us home

shivering in his trailer like mermaids
in a carnival. We watch forked lightning
over the railway track, count the miles
in seconds, take turns to dip fingers

in the nightlight and peel off fingerprints,
trying to get a perfect one. In the white café
on the edge of town, I fry chips, boil peas,
while you serve meals for eight pounds a week

and all we can eat. My clothes are stiff with grease.
The owner's mother at the sink has no English
or Welsh. She nods and smiles, chatters in German,
gives us pennies to spend, like grandchildren.

We drink cold Double Diamond in straight glasses,
smoke before breakfast. At nights I lie awake,
listen to your breathing. You talk in your sleep
but I can't make out what you're saying.

Back home in Kidderminster the juke box
in the Green Man still plays the same tunes.

Telescope

November 2am frost. My brother
on a deckchair in the back garden
is dressed for it: balaclava, socks on his hands,
two overcoats and a blanket. He sips scalding coffee
from the flask and, when he hears me
ease the gate, carefully wipes his glasses.

Just back from a party that didn't get started
I pull up a deckchair as he aims the telescope
like a mortar above Birmingham Road
at a patch of white somewhere in Andromeda.
Two hundred thousand million stars. It's like
powdered light, or sherbet with light behind it.

I give him the last of my chocolate
take off my shoes and socks and walk on the grass.

The Day the Lawnmower Caught Fire

My brother had shut himself in the garage
with the snooker table and six banana sandwiches
and was perfecting his opening shot
in the half-light from the one grimy window
in the far corner. You could hear the balls snap
even over the whine from the lawnmower.

I had just turned my back on the lawnmower
leaving it to cool by the rhubarb while I had
five minutes with *Roads to Freedom* on a deckchair.
The lawnmower, sick of being pushed around,
neglected and made to chew wet grass with blunt blades,
reached a decision and looked happier in flames
than it had ever looked. Even the grass
around it went black and smoked in sympathy.

from *The Pond Poems*
(*for Ian McMillan*)

Clare

Picture it: the short-cut through the woods,
dusk. I hear splashes from the pond, then singing.
I listen but can't make out the words.

I see him before he sees me, which is surprising
because he has three heads. He sits on the bank,
feet in the water, wet but not shivering

in dungarees and T-shirt. He moves his hands slowly
to the song. One head wears a woolly hat,
one's shaved, the other has a beard – it sees me.

The singing stops. I lean back against a tree,
touch bark with my fingers. He moves his feet
in the water. The moon in the pond breaks up

then forms again. 'I'm Kevin,' says the bald one.
'That's right, Kevin,' says the beard, winking.
It felt as if the pond was listening.

Kevin

The pond is clear and full and bright
and the ocean's a pond, Dad once said.
I'm tired and it's late, I'll be gone tonight.

We've slept all day and could sleep all night.
Dream on my love while I stroke your head.
The pond is clear and full and bright.

Through a gap in the curtains the last of the light
plays in your hair and measures our bed.
I'm tired and it's late, I'll be gone tonight.

Our first time together was dynamite.
You cradled my heads in your lap and said,
'Our pond is clear and full and bright.'

We'll no longer live by candlelight,
tomorrow I'll sleep on the lonely sea bed.
I'm tired and it's late, I'll be gone tonight.

The Harley is ready, it's almost night,
I'll wake you with kisses, sleepyhead.
I'm tired and it's late, I'll be gone tonight.
The pond is clear and full and bright.

Get Me Flowers

and when you give me them
don't keep asking are they all right.
Surprise me. Get something exotic
like lilies, if they're not too far gone.

Get them in your lunch break
and not from that grocer's
by the bus station. Go mad,
make me feel good.
Remember the double camomile
from the Half Moon Wholefood Shop,
you can do it if you want to.

If it's daffodils don't choose
the big long trumpet sort
and say I could only find these.
Look carefully before you buy them.
Don't get back, notice they're a bit droopy
and say sorry I didn't realise,
like the roses you bought in Liverpool.

I want something natural with a smell
but not freesia in polythene
with soggy cotton wool in the bottom.
Just because it's your favourite flower
doesn't mean it's mine.

Know what I'd like?
To be in that position
(I don't suppose *you'll* ever do this)
like in films when the man
buys everything in a flower shop
and she's got so many
she doesn't know where to put them.

Meeting the Family

He says something
witty
about the budgie.

They smile.
He is smiling so much
that his cheeks ache.

He crosses his legs
and kicks the budgie
into the fire.

She screams.
It is not
a good start

to the evening.
It is not easy
to make conversation

with charred feathers
floating
about the room.

Naked, the Philosopher

Pale, thin and naked, the philosopher
stands in the door of his flat, yawning.
His exams are in two weeks, it's 12 noon
and his teeth are still in the glass.

His mushrooms have left their growbag.
In his hot, dark room they sprout
white between books.

Midnight, he leans against the door frame,
muttering. At two in the morning
he's playing chess and drinking vodka,
eyes watering in the smoke.

He's the one without the invitation
but on every picture. On this one,
bride and groom either side the oak,
he's top right, bending at the waist,
reading the words on the stone.

from *14 Ways of Listening to the Archers*

5.

What do they do
when we're not listening?

10.

I am doing my Maths homework on the table
in the living room. It's Thursday. I have Maths
Tuesdays and Thursdays. There are fifteen
Maths homeworks left before Christmas.
Tonight it's simultaneous equations
at 7.30 it's *Top of the Pops*
and at 8 o'clock it's *The Man from Uncle*.
I prefer Illya Kuryakin to Napoleon Solo,
John Lennon to Paul McCartney and Tonto
to the Lone Ranger. *The Archers* is on
in the kitchen where Mum is washing up
and Dad is blacking his boots.
I can hear it through the hatch. The most
depressing programme on the radio
is *Sing Something Simple* on Sunday afternoon.

12.

Graham is being nice to his girlfriend
in the imitation leopard-skin nightshirt
given to him by Mike the American,
Justin is cooking an omelette
in the kitchen on his new frying pan
that he keeps in his wardrobe,
I am pretending to write an essay

'The Function of the Chorus in Greek Tragedy,'
Paul is listening to *The Archers*
while cleaning the paintwork on the landing
and Steve is doing yoga in the pantry.

14.

Right after their bath, the beautiful couple
kneel in front of the French windows
overlooking the white garden.
He undoes her dressing gown, she arches her back,
someone turns on a radio upstairs.
It has stopped raining at last.

Lighthouse

The lighthouse flickers at the end of the pier.
We watch it in our red pyjamas.
Actually, neither of us are wearing red pyjamas.
You're wearing my blue shirt.

The lighthouse flickers at the end of the pier.
It's the only thing we can be sure of.
Everything's uncertain
since you set alight my record collection.

I'm trying to work out an appropriate reaction,
rearranging things in my head to eliminate
all memory of the record collection.
The lighthouse flickers on and off.

Actually it doesn't, you point out, it just appears to.
You look amazing in my blue shirt.
I haven't words to describe how good you look
in the light from the lighthouse. Now you're here

now you're not. Maybe I should burn
something of yours, you suggest.
Your voice leaves me in the dark.
It doesn't sound like you when I can't see you.

Locked In

If there was a skylight I could see the stars
if there were no clouds.
If there was a window I'd smash it.

Hopeless. Switch the lights back on,
kick aside the cushions, spend ten minutes
with Colin's darts and the *Lock Up Your Daughters* poster.
Don't touch Derek's computer. The fridge hums

then stops. Prop the door open for company
and have an inconclusive game of football
with Celia's inflatable globe
then break into Margaret's locker with a biro,

find the tea money in the Coffee Mate tin,
count it twice, put it back
and write out a new washing-up rota
for the next six months in her handwriting

leaving myself out. Play with the idea
of the fire extinguisher. At 5am,
feet up on the table,
close my eyes, wait for the caretaker.

Thank You for the Postcard I Read it

A bat in the bedroom we opened the curtains and windows
the sound of its wings it flew in spasms

I can't believe the address we're staying on Horse Road
there are donkeys on the hill they lowered their eyes

jerking their tails to discourage the flies
the abbey's stone windows open the sky

on the beach we found ammonites in black stone
two boys with fishing rods cast again and again

four days of sunshine then in Scarborough it rained
we didn't go into the t-t-t-tower of t-t-t-t-terror

but saw two girls run out squealing and pale
chased by a boy in bandages with a chainsaw

the castle had guides like mobile phones but bigger
you could touch the repeat button and make it stutter

we had Winston Churchill say bomb-bomb-bomb-bomb
and a woman from the BBC say Dicky Dickinson Dicky-Dick-Dick

King John lived on the hill he built living quarters
he wasn't the villain of the films it was Richard his brother

I said you've still got your earrings on
she said I know, it's part of the plan

Emergency Rations are Tasting Better and Better

It's eleven in the morning, sun coming through,
next door's lawnmower doing a lawnmower impression.

The dried apricots were a treat, with our backs
to the wind, smoking our pipes while the huskies slept

Maybe the telephone will ring, or I'll write a poem
in which every line will sound like the last line.

This is paradise were we not intent on starving

I turn on the radio, turn it off again,
find the pencil sharpener and sharpen both pencils.

Poor Smith is missing his mother, makes pot
after pot of tea, melting snow by the bucketful
and is careful with our precious matches

Maybe I'll write a novel, a short one.

He gave the last of his chocolate to Hughes
who gobbled it and fell straight to sleep
while the kettle whistled and the huskies whined

The postman's been, we didn't have any letters.

Today I chewed tea, it was surprisingly bitter

We've been in this house eight years
and still haven't painted the woodwork.

My beard has been frozen for days

I think I'll go out and buy a newspaper

*Most of all I'd like to shave, to smell soap
and the touch of a warm towel, to hear the radio
through the bathroom door*

find out what's happening in the world.

Fishing

I cast like he shows me but his new reel
breaks from the rod, flies like a potato
and plops into the murk of Hurcott Pool.
We lean, elbows on wall, squinting at the water.

He snatches the rod, takes hold of the line,
leans out and pulls, hand over hand. You can
barely hear a ripple. Until with a splash
it appears, a prize, a pendulum in the sunshine.

We improvise depth charges from fireworks,
drop them into the pool, anticipate
the muted bang, bubbles, a thousand dead
fish shimmering on the surface.

History. Mr Mort is shouting at him
for firing pellets at Andy Gunn.
He stands slowly. Six foot two.
He's been shaving since the first year.

Two years later he moved to Australia.

Leaves Are Just Thin Wood

No, I don't read French,
do you have a translation?
I'm from Birmingham.
Let's go for a walk in the woods. It's raining.

Bring the billiard table.
I have the balls in my pockets.
Can you manage?
Here, let me hold the door.

Yes I agree, the rain. Did I mention
the importance of parks in the Black Country?
It's not that interesting. Mind
the rosa rugosas, their thorns
and the climber with the orange hips.

All the other woods are memories
preparing us for this one.

If I tell anyone she'll kill me.
No, really – a dart through the forehead.
Look at my hands. People call it stigmata
but really it's darts.

We quarrelled in the autumn.
We quarrelled about the milk.
In the morning she left, took the bed with her.

Daglingworth Blues

The Vietnamese pot-bellied pig looks up
but doesn't see, eyes hidden in folds of flesh
and can't be bothered with the apple we've thrown
as two motorbikes throttle past and, in the light
from the living room, the bats are out over David's lawn.

The book itself on the blockboard coffee table:
Gas and Oil Opportunities in Libya.
Black oozes from its pages, stains the new
rush carpet, heads for the door and Daglingworth
as tankers set out from Al-Khama,
the U.N. floods Montenegro with Deutschmarks
and somewhere in Zimbabwe the sound of glass.

The Vietnamese pot-bellied pig stares at its skin,
its meat tough as carpet. The bees are asleep,
not that we notice, dismantling their hive
in the sleeping wood, while in the neighbouring field
a fox leaves behind the day-old lamb's two hind legs.

On the Third Day

For my twenty-first we did the Mumbles Run,
a pint in every pub on the Mumbles Road
between Blackpill and Limeslade. Brains
is the local brew. It's easy to see why.

The limp evening drizzled over the city
sodden paper settled on the pavements
No one was pretending apart from the statues
and we didn't recognise the statues

Graham showed me on an earlier occasion
the art of drinking beer. You don't swallow
so much, you pour it down. If you have to swallow
take really big gulps, much bigger than you think.

The station was nearly empty, the last train
had left and he was on the platform opposite
crouched over but unable to call out
hesitating before that moment

Don't worry, you won't drown. I could down a pint
in NINE gulps, Graham in FIVE and Tony in ONE.

His heart beating inside a stranger's chest
his eyes gazing out from a stranger's face
It was probably too late to save him
A dog barked in the distance

Some people came late and joined us half-way.
I didn't realise you could do that.

Day Breaks as a Petrol Station

Day breaks deliberate as a petrol station
newspapers and expensive flowers
but you're tired of vacuum-packed sandwiches
and sordid headlines.

On the 15.07 out of Deansgate
she's reading *The Holy Sinner*.
The dog opposite smiles
through its muzzle.
Coffee, or maybe something's on fire
we do appear to be speeding
unless we're stationary and the landscape's
rattling past. 'It's been a good day,'
she says, 'it makes up for yesterday.'
'Why, what happened yesterday?'

Days without rain and suddenly it rains.
Another country, your body's not your own.
You want to go for a walk. In this?

He threw a stick for the dog in Habberley Valley
the tattoo flew from his arms
landed in the bracken like leaves.

L'Hermitage and a Bird

head back, a single drop of blood from its beak
on the concrete like a red coin. Dead eyes,
white feathers. It flew into the window and life left it.

*I keep doing that, I'm covered in bruises
but amazingly still alive.*

> Vittel's autumn gold and red. Strange
> after the mountains, the pines, snow,
> the unbelievable blue
> from the train crossing the border.

Drums, drums for the bird in flight,
a different sound when it hits the window.

Hôtel de l'Angleterre

No thanks I don't want a Sandwich Americana.
I'm turning yellow, maybe it's the noodles.
What do you think, should I start

feeling ill? She said my headache's enough
for both of us. I said what about
my toothache? What toothache?

Birds sing in French, *MASSAGE ÉNERGÉTIQUE*
on a lamppost. What a city, what a language!
I have an owl sandwich, an owl shower.

Man on the metro with his arm in a sling
does a crossword in a pink shirt, two men
on crutches in the same carriage,

a convention, perhaps. Picasso knew
some strange-looking people: *Large Nude
in Red Armchair, Large Bather with Book,*

two profiles for the price of one
and the hat's the only thing straight.
The hat's not straight.

A boy throws a small cardboard
box at a pigeon. What we need here
is a 1000 piece jigsaw.

Shoes

I could make him, possibly
but I'm tired of arguing and besides
there are worse places to be
than on the back step in the sunshine,
ten o'clock Sunday morning.

I grieve for them on the long winter evenings

First the hard brush for the mud. Let
the dust settle, then a dishcloth
dipped in the galvanised bucket
of rain water. So cold my fingers
would ache if I let them.

Jenkins with his clear blue eyes

They'll dry smeared so I drag
the brush through the blacking
like Dad showed me, not dab it
so it dries out, and brush into the leather
between the sole and the upper.

Smith with his indomitable spirit

Next the soft brush. Skim
lightly across till they shine. Like new
but not like new: Luke's shoes, size twelve.
An old towel to finish off.
See – he won't recognise them.

Jones with his laugh like a horse

Would you listen to the safety instructions please

At thirty thousand feet he cradles three roses
in a bottle of water between his legs. She coughs.

He looks at her ear, rubs his cheek on her shoulder.
The yellow one's faded, the edges of its petals brown.

She puts his head in her lap, she puts her head
in his lap, he puts his head in her lap.

He loved the towering peaks of his native mountains.

They move right to left across the ceiling.

At the Smell of the Old Dog

The cat stares at the space
under the table we burn
a pack of joss sticks
prop the sash with kindling

it's no good if she's not happy
restless   same dog
asleep on the same step
doesn't make any difference

Telescope needs a coin
to see the boat   bright sun
kids in wet suits jump   boy
cradles a bottle of raspberryade

Three girls arm-in-arm
wade chest deep across the bay
their voices carry
they're on the hill maybe

a little cold and hungry
you'd give a fortune
no   something forgotten
fishing boat, rope faded orange, blue

Apple Trees in a Gale

Under our feet the vast roots take the strain,
stand out like veins beneath the turf.

Mum gathers apples in her apron
and piles them on the ground,
Dad unravels a rope and knocks in a stake

and I hold a branch's weight against the wind
as the sky cracks and spills onto the garden.

Baldwin Road

Patches of melting snow on the sodden lawn
the other side of the coal bunker we built and demolished.
Horses shiver in the field. Dad cycles up the hill
on his way to work, haversack on his shoulder,
beret pulled low. It's his last day.
Next door but one, the John Denver lookalike
is burying something in the garden, watched
by his new dog, ears back, tail moving.

Jack sweeps his drive, sweeps up the years,
gathers them in a bucket, leaves
them by the streetlight that's still on.
Condensation. A noise
from the chimney. The photographs
on the mantelpiece pull themselves together.

New White Bike

Cheyney Road, weaving through traffic
overtaking the queue at the lights.
Our car. The kids scream
with laughter when they see me,
Gill smiles. I bang on the window,
pull faces, pretend to fall off.

The big house, corner of Brook Lane.
I'd love to live there: French windows
overlooking the garden. Now the hill.
I'll need a shower after this.

Across the playground, swerving
between groups of kids, heading
for B Block. A fifth year
opens the door. Along
the corridor, no hands. Two girls
step back. Into the staffroom,
once round the table, ringing
the bell. Margaret spills her tea.
Pete laughs, shakes his head.
Colin shouts, 'Yatesy!' and claps.
Derek's face ...

Yes

1.

I suppose it's good of them to come back
to Frank's, now that they're so famous.
They're well into their set when he stands up
and accuses them of sitting on their laurels.

Jon Anderson stares, Chris Squire
stares and Jon Anderson says something.
I can't remember what he says. Then
they play 'Eleanor Rigby.' It's a fine moment.

2.

I can't remember how we got there
but there's the four of us:
him and his mate, me and my girlfriend,
drinking pints of mild, eating crisps,

playing darts, and he asks me if, later on,
would it be okay if I didn't think
of my girlfriend so much
as *my* girlfriend, so we could all

have a good time, all four of us.
It sounds reasonable, a good outcome
to the evening and in everyone's
best interests. I told him to get lost.

Kidderminster-on-Sea

Travellers journey to the Seven Stars to witness
the equinox tide lap the plinth of Baxter's statue.
You can buy cockles on Coventry Street, fish
for eels off the Swan Centre, cast your net
in Castle Street and come up with a view
of the market, renovated clocks, gravy drowning ...

Ricky robbed his old man's meter
to pay off a dealer in Telford, there's a statue of him
somewhere. Joe got married, lived on Hurcott Road
until she hit him with the kitchen door. He moved out,
pretended he knew your mother in the flat
above the bus station they demolished before he found Jesus.

There are relics in St George's Park buried under the bench
overlooking the bowling green where we turned the tramps
on in our lunch hour. O where are you now Charlie,
shouting in greeting your name, a thousand
miles from Poland, the only English you know.

Vienna

what does
she see in him
he looks at the menu, the white table
she can't stop smiling   dark hair, interested eyes

    you look at your arm as it moves and think, mine?

this is east, look at the architecture
they got this far
                   we went quite far then came back
windows, shutters open onto the street light and cool
cigarette butts in the ashtray, one on the window ledge

close to the mountains the drunken bed

    you are complete, happiness as you remember it

make love on the salty ground
lick the salt out of each other's wounds

    they fly in your face like birds

The Poem

No pen or paper, for each word
as it comes, I drop a leaf
into a bowl
then go on my travels.

All kinds of things happen.
Sometimes I think of the poem but when I get back
I have just leaves, barely a bowlful.

I tip them onto the table, arrange them
looking for the poem.
Nothing. I keep trying. Hours pass.
It rains. It stops raining. I barely notice.

I open the back door, scatter them
onto the path
let them land where they will.

Boggle Hole

Two new mountain bikes chained to the fence,
three horses lean over, bite at the tyres,
get the chain between their teeth,
eat most of a saddle and a handlebar grip.

Boggle Hole Youth Hostel and someone
has written *WELCOME TO BOGGLE HELL*
on the bottom of the bunk above this one
in red felt tip and shaky writing.

A gang of hikers come in late, a bottle
smashes outside the door then it goes quiet
but for the talking, distorted, muffled
through the wall, apart from that voice...

After breakfast a tractor tows a boat
named *Freedom* into the sea. There used to be
smugglers here and someone wrote LULU
four feet high in the slipway's wet concrete.

Freedom is oil-grey just below the horizon
when a dog tears along sideways, tongue out,
tasting the salt on the wind, and in the first
drops of rain a boy draws a donkey in the sand.

The Science of Predictive Astrology

I'm Scorpio with Mars in the tenth
and some other configuration that means,
according to one source (though it could be
the translation) death by weapon or fire.

But we don't take these things seriously,
flames crackling in the distance, arrows
falling from the sky, pretty much as usual
for this time of the morning, we're out
of milk, the yogurt past its sell-by
and the phone stopped ringing just as I got there.

It was probably my brother
with news of how many badgers
he saw last night. The night before
it was seven. *Bring your own*
he said to his wife when she reached
for his binoculars. He was joking,
but there's nothing funny about fire.

Snow

This morning on the Pennines, the snow,
as if through a tunnel, opening out, snow
on the bonnet too, blowing up, spraying
the windscreen.

        It did this once before
on the M5, Birmingham. We were
passing through, around Christmas,
everyone in the car, on the way home.
The blow of the heater, the click of the wipers

        and all you wanted to do
was look at the snow and say look,
look at the snow, look at it.

Chez Marianne

In the next apartment the children are quieter,
soon they'll run a bath and one of them
will lie in it, moving. She comes out
of the bathroom, her hair standing,
shaped to a point like an alien.
Are you cold? No, I'm airing the towels.
That's a good idea, here, which
of these switches switches the light on?

Outside Chez Marianne on Rue des Rosiers
a beggar begs from a big man with loose hair
and fly undone who smiles like Tommy Cooper
then walks in the opposite direction
and suddenly down a side road, the full moon;
the traffic's too busy to stand here and admire it
though on the Seine it's reflecting in the water as well
so they have two moons to admire, not one.

Life Studies

I meet Tom for soup & sandwiches at Euston,
it still looks good, his twenty quid haircut, then I take
the Hammersmith & City to Goldhawk Road.
Someone said the best moments are moments
of realisation. On the bumping underground
I read *Life Studies* for the first time
since the seventies in my old Faber Selected (45p)
signed and dated with my younger signature.

O'Hara wasn't keen on Lowell and I love O'Hara
but there's something in Lowell that I recognise.
I recognise these underground stations
their names though I've never been here before.
That song by Gerry Rafferty with the unforgettable sax ...

I sit next to a girl who smells like a bag
of crisps or maybe I can just smell crisps.
It's not a girl I realise it's a boy
with dreadlocks eating a pear at Paddington
in a pink and white scarf, camel-coloured coat,
pin-striped trousers, red and black boots ...
'Baker Street.'

Alt St Johann

The children hide in the tree,
they whisper and laugh, the branches move.
These are the mountains, the trees
on the mountains, the rocks.
You walk and you walk
and forget that you walk.

The child climbs out of the hedge, clutching
a fistful of wheat, its roots thick with soil.
Chew the husks, taste the sweetness.
The cat sits on the cooker, gazes out on the valley,
closes her eyes and opens them.

*You see only half of the moon
and mist comes out of the ground.*

The cherries are finished on the tree,
the redcurrants ripe on the bush.
We sleep at the top of the house in the room
full of musical instruments. The music
enters our dreams and leaves by the gate
leaving it open.
                This, I decide, is paradise
where they lend you their shoes and they fit.
It's easy to laugh, and the children walk forever,
sleep through the night in the valley of stars,
wake with the light and remember.

Easter

It's different when we go back
without the children the perspective shifts. That
pool into which they threw stones is smaller
opposite the house where pink
blossom brings out the colour of the brick,
the back garden more-or-less an open field
with occasional trees, grass trimmed, fence
broken in places. I prefer boundaries crisp
except here, this place:
swerving territory of snow light.

The wind's picked up but if you
walk you soon feel warm.
The sheep have long hair, small blank heads, horns.
The good-looking cow climbs to her feet,
back legs first, steadying, her front legs thin
and strong. She raises her tail and squeezes
a stream onto the grass.

So much guilt today you can hardly bear it
but you do and carry on.
The door slams and the source of heat.
Two women, three, and I'm here all night
making stuff, making.
Place the flowers here. Now
look through the window.

Interior, yes, and very much out there the source of light.

The Chinese Girls Played Cards

The Chinese girls played cards on the train
from Zurich to Paris. At one point it rained.
They wiped their fingers on the pith of an orange
but it was the wrong kind of orange.

It rained on the way to Paris.
The sky was Swiss German, then French
and clean like the pith of an orange.
There was no rainbow that I remember

but I remember the sky changing to French.
Danke, I said to the French ticket inspector
with the tattoo on his arm. I remember
his careful beard, the collection of studs in his ear.

Danke. After he'd thanked me in English.
How did he know I was English? From my ticket,
my manner, my clothes? *Were* they Chinese?
They were speaking in French, the cards were German.

Bike, Rain

We have to get to a railway station. It's raining.

'I forgot you had a bike,' I said.

'I know.'

'We could try riding two-up.'

He laughs and says, as if reading from a book: 'He was strangely insistent about riding two on a bicycle.'

I try to buy a bike for the journey but without conviction. The vendor has two bikes chained up. Forty pounds.

'That's far too much. I can pay twenty pounds or twenty-eight.'

'I'll tell you what, I'll meet you half-way: thirty-eight pounds.'

'That's too much. I told you: twenty or twenty-five pounds. That's all I have.'

And we're off again in the rain, him pedalling, keeping his head down, and me jogging beside him. It's quite a distance, rain or no rain.

An old town carved out of the rock face. It's a tourist attraction. You can see how they lived in authentic colour.

'I forgot you had a bike.'

'I know.'

Spade Bucket Apple

No longer one to call a spade a spade
he calls it bucket or apple, it's exhausting

like mistaking a pig for a favourite cow
then trying to milk it in a ruined building.

February, Colden Valley

The old mill chimney brushed by a track of snow
points to a house on the hill obscured by trees:
bare trees against cloud, blue sky. Birdsong.
River sound runs through the valley.

Beech branches, twigs against sky.
Black, silver-grey on powder blue.
Green trunk old beech, old green
evergreen, part-shade, part-sun.
One mast, framed. Lines of soft grey,
white cloud, sky the palest blue.
Land folds into valley, distant hills.

Bright moss in sunlight on the dry stone wall,
bright green feathery underwater green.
Gathered damp the stone's coat.
Sycamore seeds, last year's rested here
and leaves: gold-faded khaki, black
stuck to frozen snow. And these –
upright purple stems with bean-shaped heads.

I Met my Friend

I met my friend soon after he died
down by the lake.
It was as if he was expecting me.
He had lost thirty years
but had travelled further.
We stood together
leaning on the wall, gazing out.
The sun rippled on the water.
It's good, so good to see him again,
to be with him by the lake.
The sound of the water, distant
traffic, and a heron, *Look, John!*
at the far end.

Bike Ride

All four of us for once, in single file
on the Birmingham Road, past the fields
on our left, the black and white cottage
and the right turn under the railway bridge.

It's surprisingly dark cycling under the bridge
when Dad moos like a cow for the echo.
There's no way he wouldn't have done that,
mooed like a cow for the echo, cycling under the bridge.

Just Before You Taste It

The best bit, she says, is just before you taste it.
Cary Grant, running through the cornfield, chased
by the crop-duster without his jacket.
All things must pass, everything comes to an end.

Hottest day of the year and you're stuck in a carriage
missing the winning goal, the unspectacular
winning goal. Winning is always spectacular,
she says, slamming again the door.

Something's going off in the fridge, making
very little noise, making almost no noise at all.

Shakespeare and Company

We stayed in the Marais near Rue des Rosiers
on the fifth floor: ninety-two steps, toilet on the landing,
bring your own towels, €20 more than the floor below
(but what would you pay for a view of the sky?)

and bought white nectarines from the market
and baguettes from the boulangerie round the corner
from The Red Wheelbarrow, an American bookshop
like Shakespeare and Company on the Left Bank

(with the bed under the stairs) where one night
I caught up on the history of American poetry
while the rain hammered the roof, followed by an ice-cream
from Amorino served by a girl from Hereford

who talked like an English girl in a Woody Allen film
and gave us a massive cone that we shared
by the Seine on Paris Plage, lying on deck chairs
under a sweet chestnut tree, waving at the people on boats.

Bar Billiards

Our Christmas bar billiards is only
four foot long but it's bigger

than a playing card.
Dad says you need a

magnifying glass
to see the balls. Eyes

water in the smoke
from Uncle Fred's Woodbine

as me and my brother,
Dad and Uncle Fred

edge past each other, taking
turns in the crowded

living room, careful with our cues
(the tree, the television screen).

Mum and Aunty Alice
natter and laugh in the kitchen.

You have to start somewhere.

Fifteen

Philip Aston was born middle-aged:
Brylcreem and cycle clips, a faint moustache,
like somebody's dad or one of the teachers.
Here he is in the bike shed, chaining up his RSW,
fifteen years old in his prefect's blazer.

Prefects. Roger gave us twenty-five lines
for mucking about, then we talked him out of it.
I saw him recently, called in at the farm.
He told me how they found their dad
in the cowshed. That's how he wants to go.

The barn I creosoted when I was fifteen
is still standing and hasn't been creosoted since.
Their Cedric showed me how to drive.
We followed a track round the edge of a field.
He had to turn off the radio. A good record
made me go faster, I didn't realise. It still does.

They'll never make me a prefect –
the special blazer, the badge – not in this lifetime,
hanging about the bike sheds, waiting for something
to happen, or singing along in the outside lane, eighty-five, ninety.

Apprentice

Mac runs past, a Woodbine
hanging from his lips, ash
on his foreman's white overall,
his face red, sweating. Brian
catches my eye, shakes his head.
It's only nine o'clock.
I set up the Heidelberg, load
the envelopes, roll a cigarette.
Bill the Cutter's half
a finger is giving him grief.
How's it going Bill?
Mind your own business, he says.
I hum something from *Basket of Light*
then 'Get Back' comes on the radio.
I can see Barry, daydreaming
about motorbikes,
on his bench a cartoon
of Himmler in a butcher's apron
shouting with a cleaver.
I've nicked his Stanley knife.
I'm negotiating with Neville
for the moped that I will wreck
one night on Habberley Estate.
I don't signal, take the force
of the bumper with my leg
turning right with rain
in my eyes.

The Bowling Green

The bowling green.
The shelter by the bowling green.
The benches in the shelter overlooking the bowling green.
The knocking of the balls from the bowling green.

The bowling green waiting for the bus.
The bowling green climbing aboard
the number seven. The bowling green
looking for the bus fare, searching
for loose change in its deep deep pockets.

The number seven accelerating for the hill
heading out of town. The bowling green
looking out of the window at the benches in the shelter.
The knocking of the balls from the bowling green.

Chapter Twenty, Leonard Cohen

is on Mount Baldy, brewing coffee
at 3am, smoking, before the chanting
and meditation.
                Here in Lumb
after midnight the snow is gone
the valley full of wind and rain
the crescent moon over the hill.
The dead are here in the shadows.
They are not calling out or trying
to communicate, they're not
drawing attention to themselves.

The bathroom light clicks on
and the extractor fan. It's Chris
in the next room. A couple of minutes
and the fan goes off.
                Leonard Cohen's
jeep on the monastery drive, the engine
cold. It's way below zero. In a few hours
he'll be in town with the beautiful nun:
two black robes, two shaved heads
in the winter sun.

Born in Handsworth

My blowlamp eyes are Soho Road
that see as far as Perry Barr
my hair is Yardley Wood, my head
Barr Beacon, my gut the spiral
of Spaghetti Junction, my arteries
are the canal or maybe the Rea.

The crick in my neck is Kingstanding
the Bull Ring a navel piercing
my vertebrae the Jewellery Quarter
my belly's Digbeth, my brain Five Ways
my spinal fluid's rain, just rain
on Lickey Hills, on Cannock Chase
my beating heart is Villa Park.

There's a Full-Size Snooker Table in the YMCA Furniture Shop

I stand there for ages looking at it, thinking
how wonderful to have one, to have the room
for a full-size snooker table, the colours
of the balls against the green, the way they snap,
the sound when you pot one, the paraphernalia
of scoring, the everlasting cube of blue chalk.

I hand over a wad of notes and a couple
of lads help me manoeuvre the snooker table
out of the door. They watch me ease it
onto my shoulder and head off home in the rain
pockets bulging with snooker balls, the cues
strapped to my back like a quiver of arrows.

Pilates

Pilates Jane moves like a cat
in skin-tight black, the women flow,
position to position, core muscles in place
and Gwilym's clattering arms and legs
are windmill blades, bent, unhinged,
he doesn't seem to notice. Tony
grunts and strains. I'm knackered
and I don't get it. *Men never do,*
Jane says. Tony balances, topples,

bounces on the sprung floor. Again.
Again. I'm laughing so much I can
hardly breathe. Jane says something,
I turn over: *Can't we just watch Tony?*
In the car park he's on his phone.
Facebook. *What are you saying Tony,
what are you telling the world?*

from *Riversound*
(In which Kevin is learning to breathe out of water)

※

I lie in the bath, submerge. Her key in the door.
I'm in the bath. / You're always in the bath. /
I can't help it. / I know. She adds more hot,
takes off her clothes, climbs in ...
She towel-dries her hair as I climb out,
pull on my shirt. *You're still wet. / I know.*
The shirt clings to my back, jeans to my legs,
water drips down my face, down my neck.

※

He sings in his sleep, stares into space
and sees water. We have wet towels
on radiators, water boiling in the kitchen.
Condensation streams down the walls.
I wake in the night, hear him in the bath.
I can't build the fire or he sits in the corner,
feet in a bowl, shaking.

※

Street noise. People. Try not to catch their eye.
Remember not to stare. Do as she says:
hands in pockets, eyes on the pavement ...
Sudden rain. Delicious wet. Rain on pavement,
rain on cars, streaming down the gutter,
gurgling in the drain. I stand on a corner,
eyes closed, rain on my face. She's here –

she takes my arm, pulls me along, talks,
keeps me awake so that people don't see,
people don't guess. Hair soaked, clothes.
No scarf, no hat, let it pour, soak through.
Don't wring me out, let me stay wet
so that when you touch me water comes.
Rain makes me happy and floods are a reminder,
rainbow, moonlight on water.

The Lesson

The nun points out the ones to watch:
the boy in the corner, the girl at the back.
In this class it's the boy in the middle
who thinks he's a cat.

Outside, workmen are felling trees.
A bird's nest tumbles in through the window,
lands on a desk. Inside the nest, a baby bird.
It's okay it's okay, the children say,
Brian will know what to do.

The boy who thinks he's a cat
gathers the bird and, holding it
at arm's length in the cup of his hands,
heads for the door, the nun behind him
between the silent rows of children
and the bird, as if on cue, lifts up its beak and sings.

Blue Sofa

For one hour the children are young again.
I have just come in from work
and read to them on the blue sofa,
the boys either side, our youngest on my lap
turning the pages.
                      We have read this book
a hundred times and they're absorbed,
entranced by the words, the pictures.

I'm so tired that I am nearly asleep.
The kettle boils, the windows steam.

How do you fly in your dreams?

In dreams I leap like a man on the moon but higher
and further over fields and mountains and trees.
My wife does breast-stroke, if she stops she will sink
through the air. Luke flies sitting as if in the bath
his legs in front of him, bent at the knees, moving
his hands like paddles. His girlfriend flies upright
as if in a lift. Our daughter floats in space with the stars.

Mum doesn't dream of flying, she dreams
of riding her bike. *I rode a bike till I was eighty.*
She dreams of walking fast, of running.
She doesn't dream of flying, no,
she rides her bike, she runs, she climbs.

Gate

A gate halfway up the garden,
a wrought iron gate she once painted cream
so that she could see it.

You could step around the gate
if truth were told, there's plenty of room
on either side but always

we walk through the gate, careful
not to latch it. Her fingers, at eighty-eight,
can no longer manage the latch

and her legs can barely manage the step.
Mind you shut the gate, she says
as she always says, on the way back down,

turning round to make sure:
Pull it to. Keep out the draught. That's it.

Middle age is a walk through the woods
without your parents.
Your children have run ahead.
The sun is out, there are so many trees.

The End of the World Again

Dolphin Street, Port Isaac. It's raining.
Crab sandwiches and a pot of tea
in the café on the hill, now we're back
in the cottage under a duvet on the sofa;
I'm reading *Exit Music* from the shelf
I always bang my head on coming down the stairs,
we're sharing a box of Maltesers and wondering
why we have to drive all the way to Cornwall
and rent a cottage in order to live like kings.

Last night I dreamed it was the end
of the world again and I was about to give birth
from my right leg. The holy woman said:
I want you to think of three things:
your mother, a potato and a disappointment.
I couldn't think of a single disappointment.

Rain on the Conservatory Roof

First it rains then it stops, then it rains
again. The blackbird hops on the lawn
with its keen eye, looking to be fed.
The wind chimes chime by the door,
the clocks tick in the clock-emptied house
and though the furniture's gone, its ghosts
are here: the drawers still full of her things,
the bed with the dent where she slept.

The mirror above her chair that's no longer there
reflects back all that the room has seen
and all that was said you can hear:
the sound of our voices when we first moved in
and I was as high as the window ledge
watching Dad painting the ceiling.

Me and my brother cleaning the skirting
listen for our lives in the living room.

Lighthouse III

And then stepping out onto the BEAM
a white horse as if newly awake
or learning to walk again, stroking the light
with its hoof, unsure it will bear its weight
wondering where brightness ends
and night begins. Next on the BEAM
a procession: the ringmaster brooding
without a whip, out of his depth;
acrobats; the tightrope walker, rope
suspended, threaded through
the centre of the revolving BEAM;
the dawdling clown with bulging pockets
looking over his shoulder, pushing
a wheelbarrow – he stops, puts it down,
checks his watch and he's off again;
the gambler shuffles cards on the BEAM
the dice rolling loud in the whites
of his eyes that snap into focus
(what does it mean when his eyes roll a six?)
hands of cards spill out of his pocket,
scatter, re-group, line up in the BEAM
a royal flush disappears in the dark;
a man on a bike, an upright bike
in a cap, a raincoat and bicycle clips,
you can almost hear his dynamo click,
chased by a dog, white in the BEAM
with a red collar who runs much faster
than the man on the bike
but can not, cannot catch him.
The juggler next who drops a plate
that does not smash on the BEAM
or splash in the sea, no sound but
the lingering song of the woman in red

and the music, seared, faded, released
from the vinyl, not so much music
as its memory, from embers and ash
cut loose, slipped free.

Travis Perkins

Me and Phil are at Travis Perkins
picking up some breathable
membrane. Ted is sorting us out.

There's my mate down that hole,
Ted says. The hole is in the car park
by a pile of rubble and a mini digger.

Ted's mate, in hi-vis, hard hat,
wrap-around sunglasses,
is up to his chest, shovelling

in the sunshine as if he's looking
for something. He's a big bloke,
he can barely fit. In fact, the hole

is just the right size. He sees us.
All right? he says, and waves.

Birmingham Canal

Sunday afternoon we walked on Crickley Hill.
Every day the light is different
evening encroaching on afternoon.

Today I remembered Dad's story –
playing by the canal as a child
he fell into a lock

someone dived in and pulled him out.
When he got home they smacked him.
He could have drowned.

This happened in Birmingham
a hundred years ago.

I think they smacked him,
I might not have remembered it right;
if he was around I'd ask him.

He died when he was ten years older
than I am now.

I imagine this in black and white
and the canal water sump oil black.
Sometimes I dream in colour.
A hundred years.   Birmingham.

Stand on the library roof
look out over the city.
Dad would know the names of those hills.

Lifting

Too early at the Custard Factory
for the lunch and too late for breakfast,
the towpath's closed at Broad Street, the Ikon
galleries are shut, and it doesn't look good
for our Digbeth jerry can hardware shop
but dodge between buildings
more or less opposite the bus station
for the five workmen and mini digger
laying paving in a dream, the foreman
on his knees, smoothing sand with bare hands
in front of the thirty-foot GARAGE DOORS
brick wall and, half-way up, the blue sign
>   No lifting
>   over this
>   building
the dark green canister, the red board –
a composition, a film set, abstract painting.
All over Brum they're laying new paving.

Collapse: Barry Flanagan at the Ikon Gallery
(for Andrew Taylor)

just a short walk
    from Paradise –

the hare's frozen leap,
insect metal, the Singer
sewing machine
in the hut, back of the lorry
mix the cement, shape it,
stitch the cloth skin
                there's rain and
wind but later it's warmer

Tell me again what she said
when you sent her your photo
of *The Heap '67 (1967)*

Everything's collapsing – not everything,
that hare won't collapse – watch it box

The post office machine spits
out your stamp and the illicit book's
sent on its way, the first three
chapters enough
                their new album
will be their best yet, no question

There were houses here
now there's money, private money
and they pay people to show people
how to use the machines

Sand in a metal bucket
sand from a hole in the sea

Bank Holiday

I feel like I'm part of the garden.
Did I really just say that? Yes.
She looks up from the salad.
With bits in my hair, scratches
on my arms, I'm sweating
having cut down the branches
of the lilac overhanging
the greenhouse, straining to reach
on the compost bin,
each branch the size of a tree;
there's dried blossom on the floor
in the kitchen and the hall
from where I carried through armfuls
to the garden bin out front.
Expecting a delivery, we can't eat
in the garden (we'll not hear them)
and the kitchen's too hot so we eat
in the sitting room on the settee
omelette new potatoes and salad
then watch the end of *The Homesman*
that we started last night after the cup final
(Arsenal 2 Chelsea 1)
music by Marco Beltrami (wind piano).
It's a miracle you didn't smash the greenhouse. / I know.

Spitfires were built in Castle Bromwich

1. Thinktank Birmingham 2019 / Aircraft factory 1940

Iconic the shape
above us, the spread
of the wings

*Let's hear it for the women
of the engine production line
the lathe, the drill, the milling machine*

Sit in the cut-away cockpit
pull back the lever, press
the red button
for the muffled drone

*For the mechanics, riggers and fitters
assembling Spitfires in the assembly shed*

Falafel sandwiches, mugs of tea
and a Penguin, all we need
as out on the street
snow turns to ice

*For the sunken rivets and the elliptical wing
For the first test run –
the precision roll and the vertical climb*

No grip, and we're single file
on the pavement, holding onto the rail
shouting to be heard
shouting into the cold

Panning shot of Spitfire flying at speed

2. Fisher & Ludlow, Castle Bromwich (*former aircraft factory*) 1950

Mum in the offices,
Dad on a job there,
carpenter and joiner.

She notices how his boots are shiny
('a man who cleans his shoes ...')
how he's always neat and clean –

collar and tie, brown denim overalls,
pencil behind his ear.
And respectful, they're not all like that.

'Would you like to come to the dance?'
'No,' she said, 'I can't dance.'
'I can teach you.'

Red Sky Lift

It's lunchtime, just forty minutes so I take
the stairs not the lift and head out
through the automatic doors into the winter sunshine.
In the Students' Union I check out the headlines
and buy a Twix. 'I haven't bought one of these
for twenty years,' I say to the woman
behind the counter. 'Well don't wait twenty
before the next one,' she says. It's more like
forty, I realise, unwrapping it – morning break
in the printing factory, something to look forward to,
like *Mr Fantasy* on the turntable, or Quicksilver
Messenger Service. .
                      I cut across to the Doug
Ellis Sports Centre and the art deco swimming pool.
I rarely go swimming but there's something relaxing
about the smell of chlorine, the stretch of blue
under those massive beams, the slow lane
and the slower lane, the lifeguard
in the red tracksuit.
                      The Twix half gone,
I head for the library for a takeaway decaf
then back in the Main Building the red sky lift
is on its way down for once, and only five
of us waiting, we'll easily fit in.

I've Just Invented the Tai Chi Sprout Stalk Form

Boxing Day and I'm in the garden
practising the Tai Chi Spear Form
with the curtain pole that Andy found
for me in the tip. The kids are watching
through the window over breakfast.
I'm just doing the final moves:
    Bright Rainbow Soaring to the Sun,
    Lying Tiger Diving Dragon,
    Plum Blossom Opens Five Petals,
    Celestial Horse Walks the Skies
when Luke opens the back door
and lobs the sprout stalk at my head.
'Watch out, Dad!' he says. I rescue
the sprout stalk from the fig tree
and spontaneously invent and perform,
there and then, the Tai Chi Sprout Stalk Form.
I even have names for the moves:
    Beginning Style
    Wet Dishcloth Wings Through Damp Air
    Dustbin Lid Exits Coal Bunker at Speed
    Rocking Chair Becomes Disagreeable
    Bag of Flour Explodes at Bus Stop, there are Casualties
    Rubber Ball Bounces in Dark Subway
    Sash Window Slams Shut on Ring Finger
    Coat Hanger Attacks Privet Hedge
    Windmill Plays Saxophone in High Wind
    Banana Smashes Pineapple on Lino
    Telephone Wires Entangle in Radio Waves
    Ironing Board Makes Sandwich with Secret Ingredient
    Public Library Saves City from Avalanche
    Sherbet Fountain Takes Umbrage and Spins
    Warehouse Fills Sky, Sky Exacts Revenge
    Helicopter Hovers Over Sycamore

Dual Carriageway Gets Up and Walks
'Kettle's boiled, Dad.' 'OK, thanks.'
I throw the sprout stalk back into the fig tree
(Completion Style). Now, breakfast.

5:15 p.m. February 9th 2017
(i.m. Tom Raworth)

     the night he rang me
from a pay phone in Chicago
during an ice storm

       & that time in Robert's
office before the reading by the radiator too hot to touch
patiently signing my stack of his books:

for Cliff
    after dinner –
– before filing cabinet
      with good wishes
        Tom
Edge Hill – February 15th 2001

& on the train from Watford Junction, shivering
in air conditioning
     the couple opposite might've slept
in their clothes   a flower

in his buttonhole, her hat,
his jacket round her, her head on his
shoulder &
     I was very impressed,
she said, with how much
they enjoyed their wedding day

A Thing to Do

In the midst of a family crisis
seemingly unending and unsolvable
the only book I'm able to read
is Roy Fisher's *Slakki*,
the same handful of poems
over and over.
I almost understand them.

Swimming Pool

I thought they let the water out at night,
but no. In the glow from the security lights
it shimmers blue, a ghost of itself.
The changing rooms around the pool,
doors open, appear to wait.
I could take off my clothes and swim,
sit on the side and drip dry,
put on my clothes and dive back in.

The art deco ceiling's impossibly high,
the colours half-colours in the humid light.
I take off my shoes and socks,
walk round the pool, taste the quiet.
No echo, just the heater's hum,
the tiles cool on the soles of my feet.
A monk in cloisters, I have been here
for years, I've been here forever.

There's a clock on the wall with no hands.
It is any time and no time
                          it is that time
when we were children, me and my brother –
Dad, just in from work after his dinner
takes us to the club at West Bromwich.
He waves from the café, watches us
learn how to swim, dare to dive,
our arms stretched high above our heads.

And afterwards the crisps with the tiny blue bag,
salt on my fingers upstairs on the bus,
the lights in the shops, the streetlamps,
Dad's warmth through his overcoat,
the smell of chlorine on the back of my hands.

Black Sabbath Bridge

on Broad Street, with a plaque
calling them *A Birmingham export*.
But what did Birmingham actually think
of Black Sabbath, back then?
For instance, I had long hair
which had only recently been invented
and in Brum one day with Enzo
I decided to call in and see Uncle Fred,
remembering he worked in Greys –
I hadn't seen him for years.

When the lift doors open, he's there
with his mates in brown overalls,
a pencil behind his ear,
and he looks at me,
and I don't know what to say.

You went to see Fred, Mum says.
What – looking like that?

Steve bought their first album.
We played it on the portable record player
in the barn after band practice
rehearsing for a gig that didn't materialise.

What – looking like that?

Sky Blues Bus

1. 17th May 1987 [in the voice of a 1980s BBC newsreader]

On a historic day in the Midlands, PDU 125M, the last bus to be built in Coventry, this morning carried Coventry City football team on their victory parade through the city, following their 3-2 defeat of Tottenham Hotspur in yesterday's FA cup final. The Daimler Fleetline, donated to Coventry Transport Museum just last year, was painted sky blue and converted to an open top vehicle specially for the parade. Asked for a statement, after what will most likely be its last journey anywhere, the bus was reportedly too choked with emotion to be able to speak. A lifelong Coventry City supporter, this was undoubtedly the proudest moment of its working life.

2. The impact of the Coventry bombing on the city's transport infrastructure

My mother in Hall Green, Birmingham,
lying in bed, 14 November 1940
after her shift in the factory (toolmaker)
hearing the planes flying over, one after the other
and the relentless, night-long sound of bombs:
'I remember thinking, somebody's getting it.'

Salvage from the tramway tracks was enough
to build 180 heavy tanks, but the Coventry bombing
did it for the trams.
     An abandoned tram,
blown over a house in the night, found in the garden,
windows intact.

3. 17th May 1987: The last bus

Sky blue flags and sky-blue scarves
people on a roof, hanging out of windows
climbed up traffic lights, climbed up trees
    cheering for the players
    cheering for their team
    cheering for the victory
    cheering for the dream
their heroes waving, smiling, holding up the cup
on the open top deck of the double decker bus

Apart from the bus route, the streets are quiet
ghost town
Sunday
listen –
turn down the volume of the shouting and the singing
listen –
underneath the shouting
underneath the singing
the bus is in a dream ...

They're cheering me on, cheering me on
they're cheering on the last bus home
    there's no blues like the sky blues
cheering on the last bus home.

Dog

So many places closed: the off-licence,
the butcher, the corner shop, even
the telephone box screwed shut.
Dog had come a long way, and now what?

The cherry blossom, he noted,
looking up for once from the pavement,
was particularly stunning this year,
maybe it was the same every year

but noticing it, his heart was lifted
and he decided not to be disappointed.
The journey had been arduous, the future
was uncertain, but there is more to life,

he reflected, cocking his leg against the letter box,
than a bowl of fruit on a table.

from *Another Last Word*

EXPENSIVE CHOCOLATE

There are eight pieces. She has two
and gives me one. 'Confiscate this,'
she says, handing over the rest.
'Hide it, or I'll be tempted when you're out.'
When I get back, the drawer's open,
there's one piece left, and a note
on a scrap of paper: NOT VERY WELL HIDDEN.

CLEARING UP

She's cooking Sunday lunch and I'm clearing up.
'It's ridiculous,' I said, 'you spend time
getting things out of cupboards
and I spend time putting them back in.'
'Not enough time in my opinion.'

BIRTHDAY

'You're being nice,' she says, 'you'll be running
out of steam soon. You've been nice
since 7 o'clock, that's 3 hours, 10 minutes.'

DANCE

'It's great the way we dance around each other,'
I said, 'when we're getting the meal on.'
'We only do that because you get in the way.'

SATSUMA

'I can't be bothered with this satsuma.'
'Give it here,' she says. 'Can't peel a satsuma,
can't peel an egg. We've been married how many years,
and I've made no progress with you whatsoever.'

WRITING

'I had to work on that one,' I said, 'because
you didn't actually say that. I am in fact
writing these poems.'   'That's what you think.'

ENTERTAINING

'Some of these make me sound terrible,'
she says. 'It's because you find me so entertaining.
It makes me worse when you start laughing.'

LUNCH

'Apart from the salad and potatoes,'
I said, 'what did we have for lunch?'
'If you can't remember what we had for lunch
I feel sorry for you.'

GETTING IT RIGHT

'I'll get it right one day.'   'I doubt it,' she says.
I laugh. 'It's not funny really, is it?'
'No,' she says, 'but at least you're hopeful.'

PHILOSOPHY

'You're too hard on yourself,' she says,
'when I wake up I just want a cup of tea
and then I want to be entertained by life.'

FISH

'What we need is a special pan for fish
and a fish spatula.' 'No,' she says,
'what we need is for you to eat fish.'

COLOURING PENCILS

She's at the kitchen table, going at it
with her new colouring pencils.
'I had some when I was little,' she says,
'but I was never let loose. It was always
What's THAT supposed to be? or *Where's the SKY?*'

Taxman

'Guess who played lead guitar on Taxman,' I said.
We're walking down Exmouth Street in the rain.
'What's Taxman?'

'The first track on The Beatles *Revolver*.
It was written by George who was lead guitarist,
but he didn't play lead on Taxman,
someone else did. Go on, three guesses.'

'Eric Burdon.' She's thinking of Clapton
which isn't a bad guess. Next: 'George Best.'
'You're not taking this seriously.'
'I wish you were more interesting,' she says.

Tonight We're Showing a Film

People no longer queue outside the cinema
in flat caps and headscarves, this isn't the 1950s.
Two girls are singing in the toilets, it's the acoustics.
We should rent them out as a recording studio.

We're showing *Something in the Air*
directed by Olivier Assayas. It's a good (French) film.
There's a lot of fire and dreaming.
Set in the 70s it's coolly nostalgic

the soundtrack's outstanding and everyone
is earnest mostly. The police are violent.
Well they can be, that's not fiction
and setting alight to buildings is violent.

We have problems with the lighting man.
He was up all night watching the election.
Well, who wasn't? Dreamy adolescence,
politics and art, that's not a bad combination.

Fish Street

We're staying on Fish Street which sounds about right
l-l-l-learning how to b-b-b-b-breathe my head
feels unaccountably light and when I lie on the bed
I flop like a child or a dog.
We buy strawberries from Norway Stores
grown on Phil's allotment, he harvests them
in May, June and August, they call him *Strawberry
Phil's Forever* and suddenly anything's possible.

We grate the cucumber because the knives are no good
and in the Co-op on our way to the checkout with a family
pack of Kit Kats for the cinema, the woman in front of us
drops in slow motion her bottle of wine (pink in this light)
and the boy takes forever gathering the glass
with kitchen roll, dropping it into the black
plastic bucket, dabbing the pink, as if he has
bandages wrapped round his hands.

The bathroom's full of sunlight, either that
or we've left on the light, but just after midnight
woken by the wind rattling the window
I can't see to write and the light would
disturb her so I open the door of the fridge
and crouch on the carpet with my notebook
in front of the carton of eggs, the remains
of the cheese, the garlic, the milk in the door.

Eagle Special Investigator

In Longfields charity shop on Bath Road
I find a copy of *Eagle Special Investigator*
I used to have when I was a kid. Macdonald
Hastings. In the black & white photos
he's wearing glasses like the ones
back in fashion that looked old-fashioned then.
He looks like somebody's dad (but everybody did),
Hank Marvin before Hank Marvin. The cover's
unfamiliar: mostly yellow (some red), Eagle logo,
Macdonald H. bottom right, thumbnail head
and shoulders in a cowboy hat.

I've thought about this book on and off
over the years and maybe I was hungry
when I read it but the only part
I remembered apart from the title
was the size of the lumberjack's breakfast.

'Mines for Gold' has him prospecting for gold
in Canada and being free with the comma:
I got the fever, over a plate of pork hock,
with Bill Johnson and Wally Brinks,
and after Bill Johnson's tale of the old days
when twenty-seven mules came in from Eldorado
piled up with gold like grain and so much gold
inside the banks they stacked it outside in bags:
I couldn't imagine why I'd wasted my time
as a Special Investigator. 'How do I start?' I said.

Phil and the Tension Wire

Phil takes a look at our dodgy tension wire –
the halogen bulbs flicker and get so hot
that the plastic housing melts. We could've had a fire.

It's since the electrician connected
a couple of spots to the transformer.
'It's arcing the current,' Phil says.
'The bastard,' I say. Phil looks at me.
'Are you two always like this?' my wife says.

Phil tells me about a walk he did
with Mez along the Severn –
orchards, the old types of apple.
The water was silver
and in the low sun you could see the river
flowing in both directions.

Meeting the Train

IXAT in the rearview mirror
pulling into the car park
the Brum train's late, signal failure.

Blood on the Tracks on the car stereo,
wind up the windows, turn down the volume
8.30pm just getting dark.

A man with his family and an eye patch
waiting for their lift,
the light in the ticket office window.

Your new red dress with writing on the back,
lipstick and walking shoes, suitcase
full of clothes for Switzerland snow.

Back home a bowl of soup, bread,
tulips in the vase, two lighted candles
on the kitchen table.

Bastille Day

Two lads on scaffolding in the courtyard
in red T-shirts and white helmets
they grin and wave when we open the curtains,
fighter planes in formation head for the Champs Élysées.

We sit in the sun in Place des Vosges
find hidden museums, rummage in bookshops
for thrillers, buy food from the market
and cook in the dark kitchen.

The Maigret I brought is set in Concarneau
not Paris, *The Yellow Dog* it's one of his best
though I've only read four and I'd say that
about three of them, I decide, finishing it
on Eurostar in the tunnel. She's asleep
1.20 French time, 12.20 ours.

Nightingale

I cast you a nightingale
in bronze, after seeing
Flanagan's elephant

but when I turned my back
it smashed through the window
and flew away.

I cast its song in water,
it evaporated, you'll hear it
next time it rains.

October

In Bruges we watched Eisenstein's *October*
with the Brussels Philharmonic Orchestra,
the subtitles in French and Flemish.
The soldier in the trench flinched when,
with the explosion, soil rained on his head.

He reminded me of Dad in his Marines uniform,
1943, who would have been eight in 1917.
The soldier shakes off the soil but he's worried.
And the part where they wheel small cannons
past the door marked 'Committee.'

Look at the sky without winking, you will see angels.

I ask you to repeat it, trundling our cases
over Minnewater Bridge. The girls here
wear uniforms differently, less seriously.
It's easy to imagine them without them,
travelling backwards out of the city.

Acknowledgements

Poems are taken from the following collections: *Henry's Clock* (Smith/Doorstop, 1999), *Frank Freeman's Dancing School* (Salt Publishing, 2009; Knives Forks and Spoons Press, 2015), *Jam* (Smith/Doorstop, 2016), and from the pamphlets *Birmingham Canal Navigation* (Knives Forks and Spoons Press, 2020) and *Another Last Word* (The Red Ceilings Press, 2021); thanks to the editors. Thanks to the editors of the following journals where several of the New Poems first appeared: *Anthropocene, NOON: journal of the short poem, The North, Shearsman*, and *Under the Radar*. Many of the poems in this collection have been revised, and differ from those versions originally published. Special thanks to Peter Sansom, Ian McMillan, Ann Sansom, Robert Sheppard, Andrew Taylor and Gillian Yates.